I've got you!

Dedicated to

Ayman and Adam

Since the first precious day I met you,
I held your delicate body in my arms.
I made sure you were fully supported and safe.

Our bond became strong and continues
to grow until the end of time.

I am grateful you are in my life.
I am so happy to be your parent.

I want you to hear this,
and hear it well.

I want you to know—
I've got you!

I've got you when…

You say your first word…
I am thrilled to hear your wonderful voice.

I've got you when…

You take your first steps.
I will encourage you and *keep you safe.*

I've got you when…

You're feeling cold and chilly.
I will comfort you by giving you the coziest,
fluffiest, warm blanket.

I've got you when…

You're feeling hungry.
I will make sure you have a nutritious meal,
healthy snacks, and proper hydration
to keep you growing strong.

I've got you when…

You are feeling playful.
I'll ensure you have fun activities and toys around.
I'll even join you in the fun!

I've got you when…

You are in pain.
I will run to the rescue, kiss your owie,
and make sure you are all better!

I've got you when…
You become sick.

I will make you soup, check your temperature,
take you to the doctor, and stand by your side
until you are healed.

I've got you when…

You are feeling nervous,
like when you start your first day of school.
I will encourage you and make you feel at ease.

I've got you when…

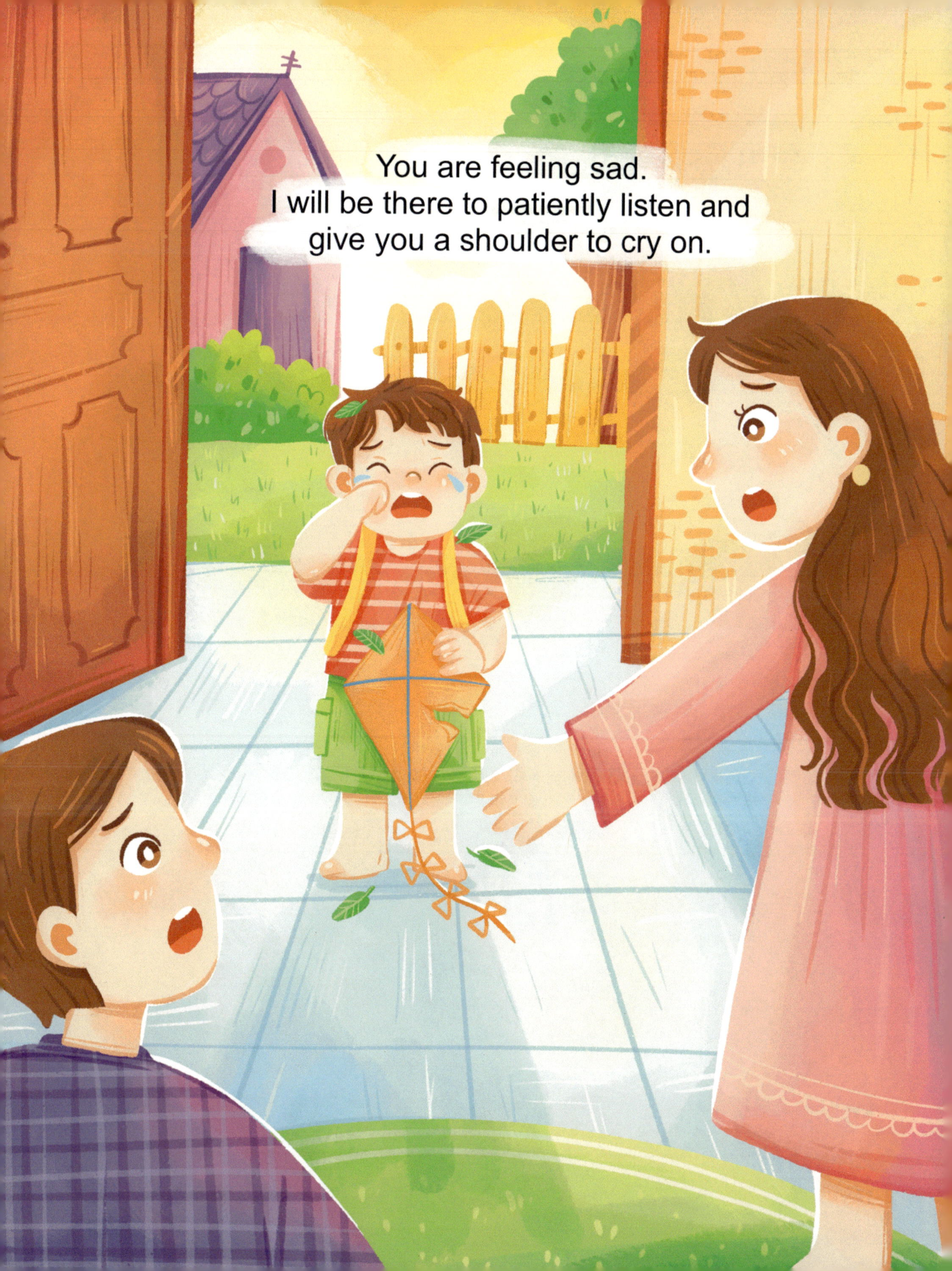

You are feeling sad.
I will be there to patiently listen and
give you a shoulder to cry on.

I've got you when…

You are feeling happy.
I will be right there celebrating with you.

I've got you when…

You have graduated from school.
I will stand tall and proud.

I've got you when…

You decide to move out of our home.
I will guide you with your new journey.

I've got you when…

You found your love
and get married.
I will be elated with joy.

I've got you when…

You have your own child.
I will love your child
as I have loved you.

I've got you when…

You are feeling lost and confused.
I will be the light that guides you
through difficult times.

I've got you until the end.

Made in the USA
Monee, IL
07 July 2026